MILLENNIUM FEVER

MILLENNIUM
F E V E R

P O E M S   B Y   J A C K   M A R S H A L L

COFFEE HOUSE PRESS :: MINNEAPOLIS

Some of these poems originally appeared in *ZYZZYVA, Talisman, Caliban, Seneca, Pequod, Berkeley Poetry Review, Barnabe Mountain Review, Five Fingers Review, Western Journal of Medicine,* and *Poetry Flash.* "Chaos Comics" first appeared as a chapbook from Pennywhistle Press, Tesuque, New Mexico.

Coffee House Press is supported in part by a grant provided by the Minnesota State Arts Board, through an appropriation by the Minnesota State Legislature, and by a grant from the National Endowment for the Arts, a federal agency. Additional support has been provided by the Lila Wallace-Reader's Digest Fund; The McKnight Foundation; Lannan Foundation; Jerome Foundation; Target Stores, Dayton's, and Mervyn's by the Dayton Hudson Foundation; General Mills Foundation; St. Paul Companies; Honeywell Foundation; Star Tribune / Cowles Media Company; The James R. Thorpe Foundation; The Beverly J. and John A. Rollwagen Fund of The Minneapolis Foundation; and The Andrew W. Mellon Foundation.

Coffee House Press books are available to the trade through our primary distributor, Consortium Book Sales & Distribution, 1045 Westgate Drive, Saint Paul, MN 55114. For personal orders, catalogs, or other information, write to: Coffee House Press, 27 North Fourth Street, Suite 400, Minneapolis, MN 55401.

Library of Congress CIP Data
    Marshall, Jack, 1936-
        Millennium fever : poems / by Jack Marshall.
        P.   CM.
    ISBN 1-56689-054-3
    I. Title.
    PS3563.A722M55   1996   96-2773
    811'.54—DC20   CIP

10   9   8   7   6   5   4   3   2   1

Contents

PART ONE—

13 Air Dagger

15 Wing and Prayer

18 Her Flag

19 Field and Wave, Body and Book

24 History, Any Day

27 Of Jeffers, 1961

28 Sunset News

PART TWO—

38 Chaos Comics

PART THREE—

57 Autumn in the Fall of Empire

59 Limb

61 Alone in Honolulu

63 Arabian Hula, Hawaiian Veil

65 From the Big Brass Handbook: Chapter 3

69 Union

70 Working

PART FOUR—

75 Climbing Vine

80 The Lie of Health

86 The Evolution of Memory

92 From an Archeology of Flight

96 In Midlife

100 Of Os

105 The Happiest Hope

For Naomi,
and for Arthur Edelstein
in belated appreciation for those
late night Brooklyn talks.

PART ONE—

Air Dagger

Sundown on the sand, and your shadow
    Tall as the 4-story condo across the highway. . . .

Dipping, picking the wave's back-curling lip, spiraling
    Flocks of straw-billed terns

Dive at each other and—no two touching
    Wings—merge, touching

Down in a line, facing the lowering sun, the open
    Sea opening

All windows. Eyes looking out
    So intently forget

The face they're in, see
    Amid curls and scrolls of wood a powerful hand,

Pulsing in the undertow, draw back the bow.
    Now to go

Stretch out thin as gossamer thread held perilously
    Intact by nothing

More than a whim, as if random
    Mercy might release a little

Pure air, not chemical vapor propelled to high
    Heaven on octane fuel, taking

Our breath away. Taking
   Time out from the rush to the cliff-edge, that

One not fall
   From same, we're here

Slaking a thirst for the smallest
   Packet of energy making its way

Amid hostile moving metal, silver-
   Tongued like the shiny track

A finger leaves in velvet.
   And those who hunger, not linger, for

What remains will know their hearts
   Shared in the open . . .

To eat, to taste, to change
   The feel of time . . . the way the birds

Filter and fling
   The air through their hollow bones.

      The birds know. Follow the birds.

Wing and Prayer

Dear fellow infidel, let's pray
    That this daily poisoned rain pouring
Torrents of contaminant crude
    Does not become the norm from now on,

Or the nightmare dreamed I know now for sure
    Will be delivered. Earth's not cherry anymore. O-
Zone's broken hymen, eroded topsoil, rising waters, and forests
    Burnt faster than fired brain-cells, quicker

Than you can say "The self's cry
    In roasting meat tastes but cannot
Touch the source it eats," fire's
    The future. Prophets had foretold it, though

Prophets and the news they carry are always
    Too late. While the plane of fire more swiftly
Plays out what on the plane of earth takes
    Time, things have never been so

Hot as we are going to make them. Circling the center
    Close to all the extremities, there's something
Nuclear going on. With the compliments of
    What corporate birds of prey, casually polluting

Slaughterers, have the time-released, barely traceable air-
    Borne gas chambers been set
In motion? Who'll make a living
    Text out of the toxins? God must

Be real
    Pissed. Torched garden, infected fruit, dwindling
Herds running for their lives; sex never more
    Iffy, and loose

Sex definitely
    Out. In less than a lifetime, to see
Birth, and death, and the imminent unimaginable
    Death of birth, O endangered

Unborn
    Lovers of the golden-headed
Tamarin, wild mustang, Bengal tiger, snow leopard, bald eagle,
    Even the pea-brained dinosaurs lorded it

Over the mammals for 60 million years
    Until a hail of comets fused
Their molecules into fossil fuel, opening
    The way for us. Thank our lucky stars, indeed!

In a world where silk is
    Thread, web, and spider, too,
A door swings open
    On a life when the limbs in question feel

Underfoot the richness of
    Generations gone
As you pass them tumbling
    Down all the way, and light

From no solid source, illuminating no solid
    Body, presses for a little while the
Figure out of shape. It needs, like us,
    A wave

Of enchantment welling up from the lower levels
    To draw it out. Inexhaustible,
The combination of enchantments possible
    In the combination of one person

With another, offering looks that awaken, looks
    That can touch
You back. It takes
    Two to have one's

Heart
    Broken. Not I, but
Erik Satie has spoken
    Through the notes, echoing oceans

Apart between the hearts left
    Unbroken. And that's only the tip
Of the hunger there must be in paradise
    For its children to leap into hard,

Hard rest. They walk, bickering, out
    Of the past into the distant
Present, on the street before the wind
    Leaves for the other street

Corners of the world, undoing
    What's been done by doing
What needs to be but won't be
    Had. Now a lunging

Greyhound on the beach goes running down
    Perfectly synchronized flocks of birds swooping
Offshore, that tremendous outstretched underbelly, outflung
    Paws defying gravity, coming

As close to flying as we'll

      get to heaven

Her Flag

On one of our long, wearing walks
down the dirt path fronting the length
and breadth of our patch of ocean,
back from Sunset
Nursery—me only half-kiddingly griping,
sorely hobbling on
                              the ankle sprained
at racquetball three months before,
and she, heartily, as is her way, more than half-
mockingly laughing me silly, laughing our loony
heads off. . . . As good as it gets.

While kvetching, I'm schlepping a sack of compost soil;
Naomi cradles and shades a potted, dancing-doll-legged
cymbidium orchid in her arms, white fluttering
blossoms, delectable yellow centers, edged
shell-pink membrane translucent as a newborn's
eyelid, her open hand shields; the same hand
at the mom-and-pop grocery will pick the battered
bruised fruit and vegetables because no one else will.

With our swaying matching swag and all her gangling
angles softened with delight, each curl and petal—part
vein, part flame—in range of the ocean's terrestrial
                                                      erasure . . .

    We have bought, she and I, a piece
                              of the same action.

Field and Wave, Body and Book

I
Now in midsummer, watching
    white wing flung out
beside white wing crossing

over spilled sewage, compacted trash, corrupt
    perfumes en route, recycling allure,
it's too late to undo

the choices that brought you here.
    But what happened
to that girl left

untouched, whose near-touch felt
    like nakedness, each word
naked speech? What luck

to have found yourself in that place and the added
    luck of the hour when a kiss is an ab-
original thing, and even parting thrills!

Then, the silkworm spins
    a yellow robe and sunbeams
strobe the drops sliding from a lifted oar

in the mineral law our ancestors' contagious
    chemistry crawled in, drifting
from interstellar disasters in a smog

of stars red-shifted to spacy blue.

2
                    O you out there,
if your lenses have sighted us, come
out, come out from geology,

sit on the shore.
        That is the house
where we were born.

What lack
        must have sent us
scattering to pick

our way in a decay
        of isotopes and a plague
spreading more quickly

now that the walls are down?
        A picture had held us
captive and we could not

get outside. Inside the frame,
        taking on a shine
long forgotten, long fore-

known, a shimmer not yet
        born, not yet come
out of geology.

3
Once there was a king
        saying no, never,
promising not to leave,

no, never to leave
          us alone. That was then, when
the future was at its most

marvelous, before it began. Then how quickly
          we come to love the moment
that had been and the moment it's over

we look for what was
          where it used to be. How little
the familiar looks

like it has long to survive, and the incredible
          hope of seeing the dawn
of credible day! How call, King,

your dormant, depressed, dispersed
          powers to a point, spiky
as the opening bars of

Prokofiev's *Alexander Nevsky*, hornet-
          sting through
a Czar's velvet sleeve, or the crack

in the ice when the first lightbeam showed
          now particle, now wave, and the huge
nebulous house of Newtonian physics came

crashing down, a sound closer
          to radiation drone
than a Chopin nocturne?

4

On such a day clearly
    seeing everyone present as though
prior to parting, listen

to sounds the pavement hears and keeps
    on hearing, music of poor
Saturday night streets stretching

the length of a sob, echo
    of a sob in the avenues and alleys fatigue keeps
open, and closes on those who continue.

Your ear leads you on, yet
    listening will awaken the one
who remembers you only

when you've forgotten yourself—
    sunlight drawing up through your striding
legs, each step's drawn water-

drop on the tongue baled up for the long haul,
    and in the single head, the scarlet
tongue of a world too wild for naming.

5

In the quantum hum of phantom heaven,
    the more we look for, the more
will exist, like oceans rolling in, importing

new climates we're separated from
    by only a film, flick of the wrist, turn
of the eyes in another direction in this

confusion, creation, the certain
    confusion of creation, portable
landscape more true than patriarchs

to their tongues, than white-headed, black-
    throated, yellow-eyed starling
songs yet to be

sung, the wayward flight of
    prophecies to come . . . The way a guide-
wave shapes oncoming swells and folds

and unfolds back into the outflung mass, carrying
    the imprint ever deeper into the weave, a wave-
length of the marvelous gives birth to one

of the lovelier faces of chaos, beautiful beyond
    belief, whose eyelid memory has not closed
over yet, whose look asks "Find me," who

whispers "Bring condoms and Vitamin c."
    With a shut-in's hunger for the bodiless
aurora to last a moment longer, tired

of turning continually
    alongside a sea-grain of the galactic
ocean swirl here below, I have read

in the body, and the book is sad.

History, Any Day

Hardly a breath of wind
sends the leaves floating

over this landscaped seafront blooming
scented privet, clover, cascading ice-

plant, all worthy of being woven
into plum-red Persian rugs as sunset-

breasted birds and bikers on the riding path
perform their last exertions.

These days, the later light stays, the farther
north moves the sun, farther yet

hotter, forecast of a future
shelter be-

reft of cloud cover, the corroded edge so
thin

you could shave with
its shadow leaving no inch

on the azure's razorblade level
but niched with trouble.

No more looking forward to having time
slow down, watch the forest rust, nor smell

a warm breeze waft from melting ice-caps.
Now gargoyle birds, pitch-

blackened feathers stiff as fossils, wash into view.
From forests that couldn't be farther

from our keeping, will a leaf be saved? Out
of a cluster, a grape?

After the earthquake half a world
away, a lone door stands

in the ruins by a rising river;
a man sits with his head in his hands.

Swept through fingers and underfoot, everything once present
giving way to headlong motion, shock

by aftershock—like a phrase waving
blind feelers in a maze . . . then it's history.

At liberty in the ruins before time
runs out, stranger

to your own door, the dust of Babel
is in the air and the bitterness of the least

in the dregs of shot-glasses! Time to see
a way toward saying what we didn't know

needed to be said. Nothing definite, but on the verge, telling
not in what direction we go, but in what condition,

as the virus strikes back, like seaweed
against rock. Speak, then; start

with spoken desire. Or will not speaking end
in deafening us? Time

to call in the crosscurrents, the fretting
separateness that can't be

you, but is; all desire wanting, tending, to end
in a shape, the way trees are

an afterlife of rain. A shine
in the high pines as the wind slides

over this mixed ash-heap, fissure, landfill
debris placed before us again. The book

has not been written
that will not end up in flames.

And let's not hear any more
about clarity. What clarity now

if not of night, not day? The aeons
without sun in the word *night!* Trying to catch

fire and growing colder
even as the long days of summer are coming on.

And that other
within you who can't be named, that salt

doll's features much too everyday to notice
being licked smooth by oncoming waves, is

near now, isn't it,
due any day?

Of Jeffers, 1961

An eagle, older than I,
Wings folded in the high bough of an old redwood, crusted
Bark thick as piling in a Turkish rug . . .
Jagged gray slopes hugging the heat
Of boulders long after sundown, and the coolness of the hawk's
      shadow . . .

Hills like fog, yet hard as iron . . .
                     No horseman, no hunter
But the winged one to scavenge
Mate, young, eggs, and build a nest in the splinters
The lightning left.
           As if fledged from heat and rock, the hawk,
Its mate ten years dead, hovered
As we walked the cliff-stones from which the house was built . . .
It shooed us—wings over its brood—away, and turned seaward
To the gathering wave-mass soon to be delivered.

One wants at such a time a summit
Against loss; to build your house beside an ocean
Is to come close
         to living in the house where you were born,
Hearing long fluttering folds of music in sundown's quietness
Drawing out the long home before breath was drawn . . .

As if the wind were engine,
The same hawk—or its offspring—hunts these same hills, crying
The same cry that never grows tired, dreams
The same rock-slides, hears the same crack and dry rumbling
Thunder of thirsty mountains in its throat; the sharp
Stabbing cries of gray-winged gulls in seagoing flight
Over heights widened for the wind-dance.

Sunset News

The traffic light's red O
does not stop
or slow the overripened
sun setting behind it

   . . .

Squabbling birds
nesting in the eaves of the house . . .
Beside the flowerbed, broken
egg's gray-brown fetus on the ground . . .
Fallen? Pushed?

   . . .

Soft wash of nozzled spray
in the garden ringed by marigolds—
Naomi down in the dark
stomping the god-
damned snails

   . . .

First feed the flowers,
then your face

   . . .

Genius in the house—
mouse that nightly does laps
up and down the curtains and refuses
the cheese laced with peanut butter
in the trap

   . . .

Of all spots to pick for a nap!—
Inches from speeding traffic on the Great Highway,
in an opening in the tall dune grass,
a sleeping bag laid out, rounded
form making no move

   . . .

Staticky music on the stereo,
overheated car-motor outside—
one sound

fueling another

   . . .

Rare, welcome up-
side to fixed fog, this bright,
bright sunshine I need
to raise my arm against,
squint

   . . .

Unseasonably sunny and warm
summer for a coastal fog-belt. Thanks
to the ozone layer's steady
burning off

   . . .

Passing the window, daily
sight of the white-haired
head of woman reading the paper
replaced by a young brunette,
tipped head held in hand, staring
inward

   . . .

Grit-sand-sea-salt film
on things under hand and foot . . . fine
skin that will cover all,
bud and root.

　　. . .

Birdsong in the garden.
Bone on the beach.

　　. . .

"You've got an infestation
of German roaches," says the dykey exterminator.
"Another invasion we have
to thank them for.
Soon they'll be wearing swastika
armbands, and goosestepping."

　　. . .

Clear sky. Eyes born to look
into other eyes, look
into God's vacant
blue eye

　　. . .

Pass the bait shop's sign
in the window: THE MASTER
BAITER

　　. . .

Anticipating the coming
rise in ocean levels, they're building
a stone breakwater
behind the beach. Wish-
ful thinking

　　. . .

I am going out now
to see my friends, the
waves, the holy
rollers

   . . .

Tongue rooted in tangy lungfuls, tiny
droplets, breathing
back the sea
we bubbled from

   . . .

Walking the beach,
inconceivable the outflying stars out-
number these powdery sands—

Vacuum the cosmos-beach
into this pea-sized poem

   . . .

The sunset is a drug
sorely missed
when not
       downing

   . . .

The Asian women on the "N Judah,"
exhausted heads resting on the backs
of seats in front of them—
heading home after work at what
laundry press, kitchen, grocery, Chinese

Wall?

   . . .

A tired woman's yawn
swallows the tongue-tinted sun-
down it spawns

   . . .

Girls at the Music Conservatory,
playing violin—
short and tall—elongate, their slender
bodies vibrating, tendrils

on tiptoe

   . . .

No need to be nearer
this woman whose air
disappears

ever deeper in my ear

   . . .

Before the concert,
members of the Japanese soloists' families
step into the lobby and bow
profusely to each other,
carrying trays of sushi and cookies.

I too will soon be learning to bow

   . . .

As news of the slaughter
in the streets of Beijing
filters down to us,
a young Chinese man in black formal wear
plays a Mozart sonata on the piano
with all the delicacy and fastidiousness
of a Viennese virtuoso

. . .

Are we who walk,
to the double amputee vet in the wheelchair
waiting on the platform,
what birds seem to us?

. . .

What's that
foraging on the shore?—fog-
colored gulls

. . .

After collecting a handful,
we grow picky
about the pebbles
we'll pick up from the beach

. . .

After A.'s death, I invite B. one day
for a walk on the beach.
"I'm from Minnesota; I don't like the ocean," he says.
I'm stymied, but glad he's retained his spunkiness.
A few weeks later, he admits,
"I wish I'd brought A. more often to the beach;
she loved the ocean."

. . .

Joggers' flashing
strides, like spokes of an invisible wheel . . .

The job of the work is to jog the worker

. . .

Sea, whispery
edge of a trans-
migrating planet

            . . .

Dog lunging to run
down a bird
into the waves,

misses, head cocked, lifts leg,

adding just now
this
        much dog-piss

            . . .

Once we had the sea
for free,

now we are going
to pay for it

            . . .

Sea that salts our sex, all
our mother
                senses thrown

                            open

            . . .

July 4th: Stink and whine of
fireworks set off from shore . . .
These people—when there's no war,
create one

            . . .

Wide open, tide-slow,
shutter-eye-
lens of the waves
taking myriad time-
lapse photographs
of everything at once

    . . .

Freighters plowing into sunset—
Once it was you leaning over the rail,
looking into the red horizon for Africa;
now it is Africa looking
back

PART TWO—

Chaos Comics

I
Heart stumbling like a blind man
fingering the *Playboy* centerfold's
braille contours beneath his fumbling

touch, connecting dots,
  like the computer's leaping
    cursor haunted by the ghost of communion,

    with a thin, cautious breathing, just a thread
  of air, I
catch more clearly the coming

onset of blind dancing
  demons in the atom's navel, moment-
    ary quantum leaps at the nucleus's center

    where he from whom we have most
  to lose, leaps, laughing.

For the dancer in the center knows
  the center is empty,
    or so full, bound-

    less, bounding, broken-
  rule that chaos welcomes, track-
less particle through a cloud-chamber.

A star collapses
  in a spoon
    and weighs twenty suns . . .

Twenty suns vanish
into a black hole, never to rise
from the horizon.

Yet we believe, we believe
we've found the smallest building block
every self-enamored age believes

it's found. Muons, photons, gluons, strings,
TOE (Theory of Everything)
stubbed on a conundrum:

"A machine powerful enough to accelerate particles
to the grand unification energy would have to be as big
as the Solar System—and would be unlikely
to be funded in the present economic climate."

Abuzz in this beehive, vortex, compost, news
is mostly what someone wanted hidden,
where eyes approach the apprehendable with all

the delicacy of a hippo mounting a gazelle,
like memory's shutter-eye
before a scene it has not

closed over yet,
letting everything go
on at once. . . . O brief

banished one in the permanent wood, harking
to beginning, bring something
back: sun in the stubble not yet

grass; dream barely remembered you've wanted
to get back to; abacus of first thoughts—child's
hunch of what's out there leaping

in the train whistle below the window;
  in the ship horn moaning in the distance before
    the days duly plod there—to their chosen

    end; fruit born before the tree,
  foreseen, but not
the gradual flowering there. There's more

of the past in the future than the present
  ever knows. The future is behind us,
    and the past is where we go,

    wherein every move sounds
  like a blow radiating
in all directions. Go

along with the notion, and come
  with me through the moonlight
    of it again. "Earth Angel"—how sing-

    ular that rejoicing
  disappointment, living
legend in the limelight, waxing

as the legend wanes. One
  night with you makes a proud man
    humble. One night with you makes tough

    guys crumble,

    while the same hummingbird
  or its descendant is at work
among the blooms gusting

turbulent perfume;
  and the highest goal of the highest
    life on earth dreams

    of outer space—consciousness
capsuled in microchips.

Would discovering we are alone be less
  or more incredible
    than life dusted throughout the galaxies?

To house the unhuman and enlarge the house. . . .

    Whatever accompanies you comes
  from that place, flying
backward, the angler casting for what's already
                                    caught.

Delouse, delouse yourself of the good
  old days, the knives gone
    dull, where you wouldn't be a cook, wouldn't

    be a cook in such a sad kitchen!

Between the ivory and ebony, blindly
  knocking at the doors, telling multiple-
    colored tales of sparks

    that, moving, also sing, like a pilot
  freed from the laws of motion, strange
attractor whose water-

mark is everywhere, seconds
  long and a home as brief
    as a wave, randomly

exploring the smallest niche
breaking down, dissolving
I, this being

singled out in one body's breath, candle-
light flickering, light and dark
dissolve present

and absent together.

How much there is to be parted from
in the narrows
and entrances we're allowed.

In the daily
dream of firm foundations where the remnants whisper
and the yellow lives inside

the shadow of the blue, here
comes a night you can never quite close
a fist over. Whiteness

of a pillow deepened by the imprint
of an absent head; eye
bidding adieu, ear

open to echoes from shores awaiting
their trespassers, human-
shaped columns, smoke knowing nothing

of sun on stone, nor of summer
with any face you can feel
ever having resembled

your own. After bodies, we like sound
    best; after entering bodies, we love
entering sound. Bodies come to

an end; sound continues, returning,
    enlarging the space passed through.
        This is legend

        among the legions of the blind
    you pause to take another
breath among.

2
I, for one,
    would stay to see
        and catch and claim

        the heart's skill to survive;
    arms for flippers, and feet
for those who cannot fly.

One who is entirely at the disposal of others
    cannot exist. Black slaves who injured
        their feet or hands accidentally

        would say, "It does not matter,
    it's the master's
foot, the master's hand."

        To dismantle an ideology means taking apart
    the apparatus of old breathing. It dies
hard, that world . . . half gleam, half cry.

What tightens the knot?—wrinkled,
  leathery rabbinical hand long
      perfumed as the past;

      what loosens it?—birth-
  blade's sharp cutting
edge, honed sharper

against you, releasing
  in the beating
      new hearts in us the god who lives

      now and as long
  as we do.

Nothing else matters,
  say the roses, but bloom
      and blood, our

      bloom, your blood; for the real is
  a mass of steel hurtling
at you and yours beneath

elm and willow shading your picnic
  where mote tilts with mote
      and the butterfly unfolds

      dusted wafer-
  wings scattering
the atomized

pollen of perception just a little
  ahead
      of our reach. Like the feel

of a form held, then breaking up
  as you pin it down; bringing it
forth as you break it up; the about-to-break

line turns, reverse twist
  looking back as it leaps
    forward, facing both ways in the data stream.

    3
  How a fragment suddenly traces
   its place in a design, like perfect
speech imperfectly

heard by a man of words who loves silence
  in a world made of words
    and unmade for the sake of words, worm-

    holes tunneling like larvae through
  one ear and out the other.

It dies
  hard, that world. The rust that grows
    at the heart of noise does not

    so easily disintegrate back
  to its root, clearing the rubble
we cling to and of which our songs

sing, making them first
  vacant, then uninhabitable.

4
Momentarily out of this mayhem run
  aground, I am going
down to the beach to gather driftwood for a fire and stretch

the airborne
  muscle till it feels inborn, though it's not
    the only possibility, and we don't live there. Let's

    approach through the dead
  movement in footprints in the sand, breathing
back in our lungs in miniscule

drops the sea-
  breeze savored like marrow scenting in bone
    a way through the undertow.

    Come,
  or go stand where white night sun, a geranium
à la Bonnard on the windowsill horizon, blossoms

faint shadows of trees made of glass, waves
  gliding like lizards over green water,
    where ship horns moo through mist and seagulls

    call with children's voices.

    Isn't it a pretty picture?—
  We had it
constructed as a dream to steer

our future by before we learned we'd have to
  kiss it goodbye for the starved
    stare of the actual, like a bird

bringing a branch back
to the boat's wrecked timbers;
while those with atomic scales and subatomic Geigers go

measuring the stellar lightshow, sniffing
their way through the black-
holed Swiss cheese galaxies, expanding

their laboratories onto battlefields.

As at Ypres, the Germans disguised mustard gas
as xylol bromide. There in the springtime
French countryside men ran

in terror from a breeze
scented with blossoming lilac.

At Jornado del Muerto detonation waves
hit the plutonium's nickel plating
and squeezed, collapsing inward,

compressed to a drop, primordial
soup from which the planets popped. . . .

In Nagasaki a man stood, holding his eyeball
in his hand . . . huge
blooming hood of radiation hovering overhead. The world,

if it still has eyes to see, stares
through the shockwave into the fireball expanding
in air where eyes, seeing the light, melted

in radiance. For an instant, everything
the same color, leaving only shadows behind on the masonry.

Will we one day see
the heart of an Israeli soldier
fatally wounded, transplanted

into the body of a Palestinian?

5
Times like these, seeing the lights
bearing down on you are real, light
as a feather and running

out of reverence, you're free
to start dreaming . . . seeping
the way ore seeps, out-

pressing the rocks, spreading the way
fire spreads the better
to curl through scrolls and sacred

laws we've been strained through, like blood
through ghosts; forced
through picture-window days all breakage now taking

pride's porcelain
tower down to a fine
powdered pit we've been

losing our richness of feeling in,
where nothing's sweeter to the ear
than the old tune done new,

where the eyes go
hollow before ego's
nosedive.

Here,
there, the effort leads
out of myself, which sometimes leads

me to laugh
myself to tears.

6
I'm not the first.
I came here like all who come
here—suddenly . . . amino
lattices studded with protein
buds, spiral
filigree of the infinite

blossoms
at the boundary where all
matter is slip-
knotted energy tied off
from expansion at the speed of light . . .

I, meaning
shut
in a shape, in a
present unaware
of any but the one
attended to of all those
possible, flickering
at the farther wave-
lengths, each ghost
twin choice leading
to branch-points forking
along all possible path-
ways at once, not only

the grid in the dust
        of points the past is, holding us
            hostage: brown-eyed
                Hebraic here; blond, blue-eyed
            Germanic there, where
    on the street crossed how
        many times running bases, we turned
            like pint-sized storm troopers
    on the skinny kid come
                from wartime Poland, his gawking
            dark-circled eyes and foreign talk;
        blocked, blue numbers tattooed on forearm.

                Not fare forward, voyager,
                    but unfurling
                    schizo-fissures
                    at the heart
                    of the matter,
                    at the heart of
                what we call "matter" . . .

                At the edge, the dust
                of points lose adhesion, break up,
                    branch apart, shatter . . .
        no boundaries but ceaseless
    entangled webs elbowing
    for the smallest niche
        to break down, mad
    hatter in the driver's hot seat
        which laughter fires
            black with meaning
            burnt to a cinder.

7
Makes one tired
of gods and their millennial bonfires;
makes for unrest without end

on the flowered garden path down
  which the good life goes along
      with the growth pattern governing

    the distribution of large and small
  earthquakes.
The Chamber of Commerce ad boasts,

"Five million people living on a fault line
  and no one leaving." Tell it
      to San Andreas; to those torn

    between body and spirit
  trying to find themselves
a temple that won't collapse.

            The problem with progress: it

e   x   p   l   o   d   e   s   !

    Like it or not,
  I'm in this
dance I wish I could

dance, oscillating, zigzag, skewed, fractal; I,
  poisoned, I poisoning
      once rich farmlands plowed barren; oceans

hissing the visible
edge of trans-
migrating planets,

while a woman in faded denim lugs groceries
past store windows
hiding and seeking ass.

Parallel to the seawall, she walks, silhouette
gracing it with face and figure, not so devoid of
lust as to go unnoticed in the street.

An instant
in her eyes and you've spent
as much time inside

her life as she has, neon
lights clinging to her like the moon
its aura, lunar

orgasm, all future
pleasure left to be felt
subtracted from all the time

you don't have, readying
us for heaven only when we're too weak
to enter.

It's so quiet there;
when you return the world seems
twice as loud,

carried by what comes
from far away in a motion
altered in the sending, altering

us in the receiving this
  contagion of a gene-
    pool with whoever else is mucking

    around; walking, like all
who walk, on water.

        8
    As electrical waves carry
  the pontiff's prohibitions, the president's
lies, their hypnotizing dead fish stares

unscrambled on TV, are we such
  lost and found temporary stopping-
    off points for waves on the way

    to becoming inter-
  locked atoms of other things? A million
butterfly brains working together

in a human skull, drum-
  skin beaten on a hill, the same
    water traveling its own beads, winter-

    long thwack of an ox
  on gossamer air saying something
like *that's not it either?*

What interests me
  is what turns
    over at the boiling point, peeling

    mass from light
  letting bone show through.
Not the pinned down, home

sweet home, but the phantom
  photon jumping orbit to feed
    what's given with time back

    into time; flame
  to be lived, out-
living flowers still to come,

the different sweetnesses
  of the single fruit.

    Isn't there a mirror of the real
  for blind eyes, too?—or in our blindness
is there more

than one face in the data gathered, altered
  by the instruments used?—each
    encoded dab enfolding

    the whole paint-skein, as each
  bit of a holo-
graphic plate contains

the whole picture? BLIND
  MAN BUSTED ROBBING BANK! Picture
    that desperation for the imagined blond

    or black gold still to be
  gotten out of the ground holding
the dark seed before meaning

splits—you
  from me, who-
    ever else we might yet be.

PART THREE—

Autumn in the Fall of Empire

There's a day coming soon and at times already here
I see it through the eye of the red-tailed hawk
Outclimbing extinction, shutter-eyeing the field below
A nearby roof, sharpening the aluminum cornice with arrowhead
Profile.

       Against the nonstop polluted pink-
Banded sky, October day arrayed like a hospital
On a hill, collapsing room by flickering
Room into the sea, generator failing, blackout
In midday, and flesh made ghostlier
In white gowns gathered at the windows,
But no one rescued.

       Exhilirating to be
Part of a catastrophe of such magnitude. In the alternate life, nothing
Is revised. On a day the earth shakes in California,
Gorbachev lops off his puppet bloc heads
Of state. Exhumed from banishment to private life, Alexander
Dubcek, cheered out onto a balcony in Prague, points
To himself, then widens his arms, embracing the crowd below.
Broken pieces of the Berlin Wall overnight are worth more
Than when standing. Welcome, comrade Christmas
Shoppers to the acquired, acquiring art, consumerism.
Everything is beautiful. Nothing is beautiful
For long. Repair, repair.

       Master mood merchants,
We are entering the era when the language of miracles cannot be spoken
With diplomacy's tongue, mechanically rolling
The gates open, then closed, overhead, the gates that lacerate, then leave you
To face the future alone. It's then you want to ease

Down, untune the rot by a microtone, feel weeks of floating
Forgetfulness come together in a moment's
Rush. Whoever leads you out will be lord of days,
The one for whom joy also holds
A dark marrow of nightmare. To see with sharpened eye
The withholding hand that once held
Forth healing as the end gathers up
Its wayward, waylaid flocks, earth-
Bound for a time, before loosening, the way bark binds a tree.

Limb

for Nelson Mandela

Let him who in a fixed moment was exiled in his own
Homeland and robbed of a future

Flush with the common sights and small
Pleasures the poor are permitted, let him

Go now with open eyes down the sunset way
No longer having to take it all in alone, crowned

King simply by stepping out for a walk
In the one world quarantined beyond

The cyclone fence where after rain there's a sweet
Tang in the air of metallic

Freedom. Let those denied
That half of the world women bring with them

For a while into this one, who see
Things others have learned

Not to see in the unavoidable gunfire,
And not been broken

In the seeing, let them be the break in the chain
Of command from Sarajevo to Soweto.

Those who have been there often gleam
In times of crisis with knowledge

Of what can happen to you there. Long after,
It's never over, never

Missing, like a lost limb's aching,
Anchoring pulse, a living thing once within limits,

Agonizing toward completion.

Alone in Honolulu

"Holding on
frailly to a butterfly's wing" is how
a burly, baseball-capped mainlander, drunken

eyes barely screened by tinted shades and shower trees
describes the locals working the tourists
here in pricey picture-postcard paradise

on Waikiki Beach, sundown on the way,
one of those blood-orange sundowns you see
a woman, momentarily unaware of her beauty,

made more beautiful in forgetting
her street value allure as she steps
from shore into shallows holding her

long hair up with a hand at the nape of her neck.
Full sails on the horizon look
Phoenician; the new moon, Egyptian.

I could not then nor cannot now tell
whether a particular pity or wholesale rage fueled
the rum-motored machinery of his voice. A low-

keyed latter-day Kurtz guilt-gutted near the end? Or abused
haole feeling a wing turning silky
powder on fingertips which have surely pressed

a trigger or two in their time? One
of those fans whose compassion extends
to pitying the poor catcher having to spring

up out of his crouch and chase
the running batter to first base . . .
But, booze-bent as he was, I think he caught it—

seeing through the gauze of floral aloha shirts, the naked
native shoulders propping up the glossy lobbies and tiki shops—
and spoke for all.

Aboveground, Day-Glo sherbert bikinis, shorts, halters—
how lovely the genetic crossover
mix of races, slim, tanned, Poly-

Pan-Eurasian China doll faces
able to bear their bodies'
burden for how long?—shopping, squatting, posing, snapping,

while no telling when the red-hot magma underground
might spew boiling lava cooling to crust, earth core's
encased old age instantly visible, petrified plasma.

As for all of us brief ones in the permanent wood,
there's a stopped cold winter hour up ahead will slow
down the rounding, ripening fruit-to-be,

holding off sweetening the pot, raising the ante.

Arabian Hula, Hawaiian Veil

Before we see it, more likely we'll sail
into heaven on a silver-backed surfboard
where things shimmer before your eyes, liquify

in your hand, lemonpeel
butterfish, harlequin bass teeming
unmenaced in the coral reef;

the banyan tree bearing up its weight by growing
downward, and sunlight baring its skin
as limb and bark. More likely sundown will be

plumeria blossoms in combed-out hair, phosphorescent
pink bikini, caramel-skinned wahine passing, pouting,
lowering shoulders into an emerald sea.

And there's no need
for pockets in paradise where you vacation
from your clothes. While shadows shed

their colored robes, others in a desert heat
halfway around the globe from home are busy heaping layer
on layer of protective gear, gloves, the snub-nosed gas-

mask of the moon. Having been on an ocean with no beach,
being on a beach with no ocean, both deserts
the same, "This ain't hell, but we can see it

from here," where all is covered, hooded, seared.

Lovers here learn slow
deep breathing, fingers beating their bodies on the one
drumskin; the beating resonance from

red-crested cardinal breaking the rut
at our feet, peacock's cry, ringdoves' raucous
hoot in the shower trees. Is all this a language

we'll be able to receive? a whistling
in the dark? or a fleeting
joy in getting details of the approaching

twilight right? Sometime soon,
if defying gods with a good
deal of gaiety makes a leaping

spark beyond us, kicking out
the jams of the given, we just might see
for once Arabian hula, Hawaiian veil.

From the Big Brass Handbook: Chapter 3

Attention, shoppers, this is your wake-up call
for the annual festival on the fault, the high
and dry golden land where sunny skies are no longer
good news and Christmas come again is more than ever
an ambulance wailing bargain-hunters on like horses
led through burning stables.

                Watch that glittering
siren whip them to frenzy down the warm burgundy
aisles, past the stacked culture on the counters and the piggy-
backed counterculture remnants on the racks. There,
we've trashed your toys and those cozy
glass houses of worship, theater booths where you play—
if you pay enough—any part your heart desires.

With the day just begun in millennium fever,
is it any wonder spending comes
to feel like a carnal rush, spreading delicious
fire from the hand?—like pleasure committing
arson in the dark. You'd need to be in *samadhi*
to ignore the omnivore air-
                      waves running together
ads for dogfood and war news. So wanting
to be good while needing to be greedy; decrying
poverty while reaping its profits; watching
swollen clouds hopefully
                 pregnant with Buddha
fade away to imminent thunder.
                 Without Buddha,
you're befuddled; without Jesus, a mess.
                   In whose hands, then,
place the remaining time folded up like a genetic magic

carpet waiting to unroll and be made
touch, sound, taste, sight, right
                              down to the molecular
seafloor-smelling amniotic
soup we bubbled from and threaten
to bomb our way back into?

              Or did you expect
quick clean wars
won miraculously with no one's sons
and daughters in them? To destroy so much
at so little cost to oneself
and not feel what it's like
walking toward the future and sensing you won't—
and neither will your children—
live to see it. The path of the light
going out from those eyes, the urns
full of ashes coming in from the front. From the many
myths the archetypes play out in every instant, go ahead,
pick any lineage you like. And better add
miracles to the new world order
                    list of endangered species.

              Under the borax-blue
dome of heaven's harem, Shiva and his dancing divas
may be sitting this one out, but our toys
are on the table.

              If you're going to make war, make it
the best money can buy. In the job of reducing
chaos to manageable numbers, is it any wonder
that those for whom smokescreens are stock-
in-trade use words as one more weapon?—convincing you
you're freest when brave, and bravest
                              when dead?

And just as there's no law
against being lucky, you're better off
asking for nothing, so you'll be sure to get it.
In the Korean War, Chinese soldiers greeted each other:
    "Hello,

           comrade, are you dead yet?"

        Don't you sometimes wish
you could return to the bad dream you just woke from,
because the one you're waking to looks worse?
First, wreck and slaughter,
then penance and tears, and the prolonged
waiting for history to smile mercifully on those who lay
on the bed of the once-
                    upon-a-time lovers
now a filthy cot down the butcher's ward. . . .

Some day or night, each will hear the moment
terror enters a woman's laughter, prelude
to being forgotten even before finished
being seen, heard, tasted, touched.

        Listen, we take the raw
out of war; we read you
the cosmic riot act,
           then defuse it. We keep the fear
bristling in the twisted bodies
under foreign fire from reaching
you, so that no one need see
how much bad news they'll have to endure
before the unbearable arrives. In all
the continuous chance-creations of its passing,
time is the telegram
              you are being sent;
on the crater's rim,

the trade winds growing
                         heated as the motive
that keeps the moment's
                         crisis kicking, plays on.

Union

The dacha is closing early
this summer: evictions by the score.

Couldn't happen
            to a nicer bunch. . . . So great

in the ruins has their anxiety become,
like antique dealers watching over

their store of hardened death,
playing the game which has the knack of humbling

you just when you think you've got it
licked, felling you low as your father felt

under the lash called "working for a wage."

You can't hide the ugliness
by putting earrings on a sow; even less

clear is the curtain between
realism and the actual.

In a swelling surge, freed libido goes
on ahead, where the familiar cannot long

survive. Like a pulse with alto-fever, a laughing
loon's lament, alone as a monk munching blossoms

among the last pollen-bound bees,
the century's experiment in bureaucratic

honeymoon is ending. The party's over.

Working

If not aloft
in spindrift like surfers riding out their combers,
nor screwed into some foul-smelling gastro-

intestinal sewer from hell, then somewhere
in the pipeline between I'll work today, make mortal
small-talk with the axeman. In the remains of the broken

sum of things this morning's predawn hush predicted,
you could smell the mood, like mold, the recipe
stir within the ingredients, coming

on in the distance . . . bird-hush, leaf-hush, open
language of space to move in . . . clouds, rain, ocean . . .
the oncoming on-

goingness of it all. If only I could keep
my lenses dustless enough! While we watch, bemused by
their shape and color, the birds move in

to strike, beaked color backbiting
beak for a quick bite at the feeder.

Even the trees are working
green motions, and there's no dearth of light
for shadows to live in. Shadows live,

and though light's not exactly what they believe in,
shadows live
                    on nothing else.

Would being as fully present be sweet
as having nothing but what a child seizes and makes
do with?—the way this morning's free-form

roving hand-
            ful of immensity raises the level of its low
threshold for the given? And risen, I

am relieved at my ongoing
wakefulness working
its itch, and welcome

even that doubt exists, welcome
density's molecular recipe for velocity. Today's
is best, and of today's the best remains

the oncoming beating heart of you.

PART FOUR—

Climbing Vine

I

After fifty, about ready to abandon the rainbow's white lie
For approaching sundown reddening the elephant-toed foothills
Before sepia darkens with its falcon's hood;

Searching for what still breathes of those who've gone
On ahead into the piled leaves blown out on the rim where all cries
Die down, it's as though everything you possessed

Had escaped you, and it hardly matters
If it all stayed away now that the dead are
Equal to God, who is also dead. In your days diving

Deep, how perfect a plunge that carries farther
Than what plunges ahead, and a clear eye
That glances both at once

Back to goodbye and forward to the glow
Astir in the foam-veined curls of a wave folded
On the inner curve of its breaking

Over the solid that we are
And wear for a while, wearing
Out our welcome? Our cells

In the same breath
As they build, break down
Into hordes of tumors, anti-death engineered to breed

And raid and run amok like genetic guerillas.

Whomever, therefore, a steady diet of despair exasperates
Into a leap toward the Absolute,
On the way make a bed

Of blossoms for the fruit—without our effort—
About to fall. Or is it only women
Are equipped for closeness

Being that what they carry
Cannot be carried closer?
Then listen to how the whole night hangs

On a barren woman's sigh that's as much child
As she'll ever bring forth. Diminishing
While breeding, dying while expanding,

Remember in boyhood the burden of trying to feel
The mind through the body; with age,
Feel the body through the mind? . . .

How something so fragile can hold together; how
The fact of death makes it a world
Of instantaneous, irrevocable choices.

Otherwise why not abort this virus in vitro?

2
Gripped in the belly
Of a fit of laughter not so much
Laughing as a fighting for breath, welcome

To the whining '90s, where everyone is victim,
Abused just by being here; soul breaking down
Into visceral, vulnerable meat and bone.

Victim: if not in middle age, in youth; if not
In youth, in childhood; if not in childhood, then at birth;
If not in this life, in some other—the tireless draining

Drag of suing for redress of wrongs foreborne, fore-
Suffered, forgotten, but not long
Before the dormant, miserly

Minted grievances are grown
Ripe for picking from the vine
Whose each fallen leaf shrinks

Around the final universal biological grief.

3
As the eye in the barest landscape will not rest
Picking out an image of its survival,
With the same eyes

That look on the moonscape of a plant, the sunspot of a bee, see
The hollyhock's climbing
Clustered rows of eyes shine for you like your children's

Eyes, or else see
All night run down the clock and the cloud's gouged, cast-
Iron lining of a shark's gut; run

Down from silvery nets the moistures not dried up yet, which drool
Thirstily down, weaving an infinite
Skein of bile to heat to the melting point.

If you have a rift
In body or mind, it knows—
And goes right for it, leaving

No wound unscathed, no claim unmocked, no cry not
Knit into bone, transplanting marrow.

4
Slack, vague, diminished, having less
And less need
For a name, how will we

Look into those same fallen faces
When they are ours, and memory no longer
A lilac on a leash, becomes the humblest

Bare element this side of the moon.

In night, when earth works out the days to come,
One can't be anonymous enough. One can
Hide, be hidden, hidden

5
But not free
Of gallstones, *E. coli,* a marriage of

Metal and moisture rusting on the air
As each summer brings a summons

With it to exceed
The last, each in a more urgent tongue

Even the illiterate can understand, rich in gifts, in danger
Richer yet. Seasons of rust that lengthen

The blade with which one taboo-crazed cannibal
Testament holds hostage another to own the god

Who makes the timber and the iron grow.
It won't be long

Till we have Auschwitz
Appraised as architecture, that ashen

Dry run-through for the Last Judgment.
And the magical, serene childhood—which of us ever had?

Come winter, cold winds will stream where oak leaves have been,
And we too will have moved.

The Lie of Health

I

Drowsy, dizzy, dopey with flu . . .
and out the window one of those hours-long, slow-soak-
ing madras-bleeding sundowns that come earlier in lilac

late November, turning to silt
whatever you may have put away to savor
later under the ground your feet find

difficult to keep
their balance on. Twilight in the deep
burnt wood and briny sea odor; on stalking

legs, loose roots that make walking
a wandering story the warm body tells
to the hard ground.

      From a height, the sea
right now would look like it was rising, all windows

        thrown open at once.

Any second now birds, strewn
like breadcrumbs on shore, will rise, mass, lock
together in fluid flying jig-

saws tight as an Escher.

Perfect
fit of having no ties, *being* the weather.

2
Yet how much that does not love you lies in wait, slow
siege of virus tucked in the lymph nodes, that doesn't kill but keeps
the host alive as source of the feast.

Abdominal abyss,
as if no summer had ever penetrated with its caress,
no pleasure ever run

through your own wiring.

Walled in, a wall all eyes
of recent dead who made you and whom you'll add
your eyes to. No voice. Oblivion, its withering wide

eyes open. Let's not
all burst into tears at once, but the isolate
shame of illness—slow solitary stripping

down to trace
elements in a breeding dish—exposes
the lie of health: the suntanned surgeon

eaten with tumor; arteries of the heart
specialist tennis buff clogged with plaque.

One more dwarfed, outmoded mythology
not immune to mockery, the kiss
of death to "truth."

3
Alone, alien, cut off, blithering mad
carcass beneath the glaze, soul's thread-
bare storefront, and just as bare-

assed thin as when bathed and cleaned, cherished
by a mother who would disappear
down the sleeves of the grass. How eager

you were to make earth leap
higher, quicker, for her deeper rest!
                              How often believed

even blind she could see
right through you.

Only now slowed down enough, only now
sunk deep enough, do you begin to feel
what was felt for you.

The weather is our mother,
and the seasons true
time travelers—spring, winter, summer, fall—

breaths holding
the oldest, recurring
rhymes of all.

4
I don't know what's got into me that awakens
the taste of old fasts and thirsts—my preadolescent
antifeasts—alerting

nerve-ends to the scent of prey. The first
raw food must have been a supernatural thing.
Now these meek, cold,

slavish days coming apart
before our eyes are preparing us
to disbelieve what we have seen

and to believe the incredible.

5
There's a mind in the blood
that flows wherever blood flows, heated
passage melting down the fat

content of one more fatal notion:
that the infant body is at home
and the world helps it;

that, cry as we might,
the tighter the cage the sweeter the song goes straight
to the heart. Melting

made faster. It must be
in order to feel the rare, reviving
fluidity of the body that we fuck, prolonging

what's worth plowing.

6
Yet why does there always seem to be a team of trained
advisors wherever there's torture going on? Such
sensitive torturers, brutal victims . . .

Why does a violinist from Pinsk pick up a gun
in a righteous fit of Old Testament fervor, convinced
he's King

David? For those who have known only defeat, is this
redemption at last, true conversion, miraculous
mutation long promised from the source?

Does being dangerous, if only
for a second, annul every law
but its own? One more way

off the calendar, across borders, breaking
new ground, new ways to breed
in the unregulated wet-lab of the brain a more pacifying,

purer endorphin, "the morphine within"?

7
In the last decade of the twentieth century,
for good or ill, rest assured
like the serpent you will not die

in your original skin.

Dusktime, ebbing hour between
dog and wolf, carries on a beam
from eye to eye day's last

runners into the future.

Even in those sad awestruck eyes at Lourdes,
there's a beseeching, searching hope for one last
embrace by something never loved enough while it lived.

The nearest, inmost, most arduous to seize
can take a lifetime to be touched
by the warm beam, ecstasy, in the solar plexus.

Dusktime, ebb
from dog to wolf,
and prisms in the spider's web,

juice in the fruit, gold in the ore,
oil in the sand, water in the rock. Here
comes a lovely girl strolling past on the grassy footpath,

as if from the castle of her youth
surveying her kingdom.

8
Of those who will not make it into the history books,
whoever now weeps for the solid
that we are and wear, wearing out

our welcome, may sickness be a submarine
way for them in the gale to clear—through inheld
breath, backed-up bile, wasted words—

a space for the buoyant, air-
borne seed that flowers

               where it floats. . . .

9
Be like that stick-
               figure insect in the desert,
cuticle-sized, bent forward, rear-end up, inverted

frame collecting night's moisture
until, from its top, massed weight rolls
down a single drop

of dew at dawn as it dips
its tiny
head and drinks.

The Evolution of Memory

Beginning in sequenced odors—electric
in the air: hot sand fused with cold sea water,
August downpour like tumbling lumber—

you can sense in this summer summers
  no longer here in the sickly sweet
    milky reek, flowering hedges,

    and a luring, wafting, wavering
  melody drawn down aromatic avenues, the rain
like a long forgotten faith

landing on its feet—running,
  reopened, rank as the drug called "tradition"
    smelling of deep time and religion—

    tugs without bottom, and foam wiry as your nerves
  whispers you home. You can almost
taste the chlorophyll in the air, eddies of

odors dabbed on the pulse-points:
  floral, mulch, minty, melon-scented
    grass opening a doorway to the sea, inhaled so far

    back in the throat you're tasting it
  before you've tasted it, genesis
grounded at entry level.

2

Not the sunless winter we enter,
  nor the baby-talk babbled in dawns left
    behind, that don't rescue anymore,

    but in the instant
  stimuli that stir the nerves, absent
soma that steer the brain, there's the quick

quenching flight of a drink through thirst,
  as in our predator ancestors on all fours,
    for whom tracking the precise

    sequenced feces-trail of bison and deer
  enhanced chances for survival: a stool's sulphur
alerted, musky spunk aroused. . . . Not for long

the peace of feeling at one
  in the presence of creatures
    not now in sight, who were, now gone.

    Deep down in the humming hive, bees,
  jacketed furry pods, busy
before they forget how to burn, procreate

faster than they perish. The wind will do the rest.

Pursued by carnivores, hopped on adrenalin,
  linked molecular messengers unravel the steaming
    knot of vapor into single threads, deciphering the mess

    into reeking message in the braided stream: peptides—
  the frantic, feel good pheromones—
triggering gut strings down to the metabolic

furnace, converting matter to living
   fuel, trimming the lag-time between fight and flight
   whiffed in a piss-sour

      twist of air. Early humans must have secreted a stench
   so putrid predators would be repulsed . . .
From fungus to lungs in leap-

      frogging aeons.

3
Now that receptors that fire emotions—insulin, endorphins—
   are found identical
      in us and rats and protozoa, have we

      miscalculated what other forms of life can feel? Why
   evolve the chemical ingredients for opiates
if they are not feeling creatures? our partners

in pleasure and pain? Why pain-
   stakingly calibrate a chemical computer in each
      of its billions of cells to produce an enzyme

      with no survival value? Whereby
   do secretions from the scent glands of animals—thick,
honeylike civet from the nocturnal Ethiopian cat,

red jelly musk from the gut of a deer—arouse
   in us sexual desire? Scent liberated from its animal
      base into steroids, aphrodisiacs, liquid memory.

4
What feasts born of terrible deeds
 delivered us here? A grammar of genes, mutating
meat of generations. Mute

as epitaphs. Mute
 as those whom you did not let know you loved
  while they were living.

 Now microchips make up the strings of the lyre,
 and no one to read us to ourselves
but us. Who'll spare us

the nostalgic history of our little sound-
 bytes and the sting
  of those astronomical numbers? Who'll lay for us

  bare at the center of the chromosome circus the particle
 of purpose at the center
of the solar furnace?

Can that which is made of code
 know the code
  it's made of? Or follow the chemical compass, cool

 down, collapse
 further, down
to densities where stars and all things—

no matter how far
 in diaspora
  from dark matter's gravitational magnet—

   are born?

5
A thousand times more cells in the human body than stars
  in the Milky Way roam through space,
      begging for eyes, a face,

      and nights chorus their recap of ghastly days: blue-faced,
  swollen-bellied children iced with nerve gas;
bereaved young mothers instantly aged.

The fix we're in: to say "here"
  and have already
      said too much. . . .

      After this, we'll never be innocent any more.

        6
      Not having much
  to go on, not knowing which
is which, cause divorced from effect,

there's a thread
  twilled of seasons running
      through us and the birds

      from their migratory clouds—
  feathers, tufts, quills, plumes
aflutter—bearing down,

taking bites out of a sea tasting of all the tongues
  that have tasted its dirty
      white foaming Arabic lip at the tide-line.

Through what dint of fervent,
  foiled desiring the opposite of their condition
did the peoples of the desert evolve their flowing

script? And for those with a taste for that remote, most
  aromatic of odors—longing—
    which bears no fruit, a moment's

    elementary particle, too short-lived to leave a trace
  in its nuclear nutshell, contains
enough longing to lavish on what we're about to lose—

the spacious green air we love best
  because farthest away, already too far
    gone to believe anything behind could be our future.

From an Archeology of Flight

From far back—the beginning—we'd hoped to witness the end
    of the century's long buildup for the blinding
showdown and feel the dread drawn out
    in the cadence of countdown
die away before the death wish
    that at the last, like sleep to the exhausted, comes
most welcome.

        Then might the secret knowledge known
in common songs—how love laughs at laws—
    for once draw breath,
and more new than ever fly us
    to earth's first seasons as to our first parents,
not with their names upon us but with their tides
    within.

2

        But I have forgotten,
as so many have forgotten, the fright and splendor of that time
    history does not prepare us for. . . .

Instead, I see a stealthy schoolboy in the breath
    of bygone seasons step out from the stifling schoolroom
into the empty corridor and, though knowing nothing of flight,
    but in his bones and nerve-ends, as if a bowstring drawn back
tight by earliest ancestors and he the arrow, take off
    over the stone floor like warm oil pouring
free and he swiftly running, given up
    to secrets of the air that a leap leaves
further out of reach. Like a fisherman's cast line reeling

distance back into his legs, making space
part of what circulates within . . .

Daily running as practice for flying;
flying, practice for breathing.

3
And just as that boy's lust without object, desire without a goal,
boils without quenching, so do his pumping
heels sprout no tufted fringe nor scales slowly
feathering a wind on the verge of
lift-off. . . .

Apprentice of the air, at night dreaming
the moon—inert, dead crater—does not console
but colonizes those who go on sleeping
their childhoods away, he soars
to reach the rare
language of air.

4
That furtive, restless boy sped
as though pursued by hounds that fed on
slow awakening things still bound
to the spot where they stood and stared.

And those already on the wind-road, the birds, what were they
before they were scattering
songs darting overhead?
Did their genes bear
keener eyes, swifter jaws,
those saurian reptile fossils
pressed into the limestone quarries at Solnhofen?

5
What wouldn't he give to be there
    in the aeons-long blink of a geological eyelid
and see the scale-clad carnivore—leaping, slashing,
        cornered on a topmost branch—draw out the ragged
leathery limb that had dragged it there, and watch it
        fall, stretching its aching
utmost to the hinged, flapping finger spun
        from the dawn of thwarted appetite and fear
breathing in a huddle nearly to vapor, vapor taking wing . . . watch it
        born from the air, outriding terrestrial terror.

6
        Did fear make those feathers?
Is the disappeared *T. Rex* not
        extinct, but with us
                        still—dwarf-
winged, hollow-boned—long since stripped
        of bulk and weight, its armor-
plated tonnage ground down
        like granules from a lens, out-
fleeing origin, streaming farther
        and finer into weightless future? Or is it flight
toward origin, where gravity's pull recalls, re-
        grips, compacts farthest flung
                        atoms in its reigning
reneging fist?

7
Make way for the bird
        which heeds the call: be a tool for brilliance. . . .

O hidden source, will what has called us, too,
    out of nothingness to witness the secret
wing stirring in the heart of things, will it show us
    what we might yet be? When the rule of the creature
who asks of the source "What direction for me?"
    is pierced like fog
by sunlight that no longer caresses nor cares for us,
    what trace, leave?—in what face, live?
Or do we live
    to enrich the awareness that is the eagle's food,
eagle white and black,
    its wingspan, endless space?
Are we food in the eagle's beak
    through which it knows and renews itself?

8
Outside, above the cliff, flocks of foraging gulls side-slip out
    of the reach of gravity, lifting
closer to blue in their black and white squalls.
    In green grass so new it's almost blond, lovers
feel the pang before separation sets in.
    In limb, in language, desiring
a diviner ditch, a deeper, more ancient sea-odor
    mixed with new-mown fields not far
from timeless, they blossom full-
                        blown on the thorn's crest,

        as they flare.

In Midlife

I

               Poised on things dissolving, green
Going to grey in the wilting ozone, soft
Summer breeze pierced with autumn. . . .

                                      Into it, lines of rippling
Pelicans—zippers in flight—with their long craning necks
Stretch and plunge.

                         With them I am
Leaving what I'll soon look back on: day dark by five,
Sunset rust, coast eroding an edge of substance, moon
Wrinkled as the skin on warm milk cool-
Curdled in childhood, sliding
Shut, a distant place crazed
Castaways call home.

                     And no more
Solid than a shadow, night stretches out, spreading
Like a laboratory laboring toward the infinite. . . .

2

               In nightly oceanic thunder, in a drunken
Neighbor's pounding on the wall, in bullied
Brain cells chugging to a standstill, so much of
Memory is washing its hands of us without regret.

But doesn't there sometimes at low ebb come
To that long elegiac look from birth, contact
With the forces of renewal in a flash-

Glimpse of the flame each feels themselves to be
For an instant, much like a vain, vengeful god
Will sometimes come

Suddenly to his senses?

         3
   Mind creates the world
Body is born into, inhabiting
A mouth for pleading and feet for running
Away. There's nothing in store for anyone here
Expecting to stay.

              Under lock and key, the best
Kept secret of both worlds: dying while expanding . . . flaring
On a screen the size of the horizon,
Then fading. This flaring and fading
Heartbeat is living witness against history lasting
More than an instant.

            How then live in it
And not gasp, head down, lowered in slow descent into your own
Entrails, with no beginning, no

         End, everywhere
         Middle, the center's
         Emptiness oddly bracing.

        4
   In the years before 2000, we have begun
Breathing—in herbs, in plants, in the rare wonder-
Working bark of vanishing trees—the grand, ground-

Zero incineration of the densest, most fragile
Medical library on the planet,
Faster than we can read its uncut pages.

                                        In what is going
We see what we are in for: feeling
Allows the image; image does not age, not from far
Disasters to the local ditch where the hard-
Driven bodies hit, some crying out
Confessions like caught
Birds keening to be free, some like free
Birds crying for the cage.

                        5
        At midpoint, it holds you,

        The unthinkable
Just waiting to be news that someone doesn't want
Known; the rest stays
                        hidden. . . .

        At midpoint it holds
You like a photograph, holding
Flesh in place; part
Dream, part smoke, less
Than dream, less than smoke, more
A dream of smoke with the dust
Done talking.

            You follow like the blind
With only a voice for eyes, because you cannot see
                                the end. . . .
        Night reaching back so long ago,
In no way could you have imagined it yielding

The coming on of day, birds whistling away not in order
To be remembered, gray fog lifting
To green in brine-soaked, grass-scented
Air, poised, in mid-dissolve.

Of Os

In growing older, one needs to travel far
back, and farther still in order to touch
a pure source of happiness and sorrow. . . .

And sometimes as though not yet over, like dust
that has not settled since the day it was stirred—it comes
on a tide moving up from the depths

into a sun that colors even the shadows, swirling
motes taking all the years since to come
into focus. Alive from somewhere far

behind the eye, farther back than contact
lens or cornea, allowing us to see, but itself
not seen, a residue of cloudy light

like smoke that remembers it was once
human. Not to say this is the way
back, but a further carrying

on of what you had thought
ended. Sometimes the trail is shiniest
where split, and in the cavity there's a little taste of

flesh between the teeth. Memory may sting
like a splinter but still recall
now a living smell, now textured taste

passing the heaped herbal stands
along the wide avenue. Stay, and any minute will trail
off to shaded streets, bumper traffic, shoppers teeming

like rainbow salmon rolling over in the saltwater tanks,
prism-aproned merchants plunging their arms in up to the shoulder.
The wet street sweats electricity and iron.

2
Behind the beefy deli windows of childhood
there's an aromatic amber glow . . .
within, a huge uprooted stump

hung on a hook. Plow
made of meat larger than a human head. Could that be
a cow's tongue

raised from the mud? Bereft
of a mouth and deep hollow of a jaw
as a boat's prow, beached, is bereft of waves?

On the steel rack, the gross, coarse-
grained bulk making you savor
your own tongue's taste-

buds tasting themselves on the raw street, self-
meat one eats with every meal, one
more awakening

mouth in the greater hunger,
one more glimpse of the fat
red-faced butcher scrambling

toward you, holding out as if for inspection
in his blood-soaked apron a ham hock—or is that
a hand, severed at the wrist?—running past. . . .

3
To see, smell, taste such sights
is to have one's appetite
spoiled for good, is to have the dead

live in your head, set
the teeth on edge, push
the chair back from the table and empty

a space the body vacates, bowels
void, throwing
open a widening, airy

atomized breath alongside you
like a twin, weightless, ever
since in the making. Not the child

adults imagine and long to be, but your own
other, holding out a future
though you don't believe in tomorrow.

As though your childhood was not yet over . . .

4
            Only an angel

could weigh less, whom we have yet
to hear from: the scarecrow Mister Z, unfinished
Angelus Dubiosus—wavering, winding El Greco, barely

corporeal body, a budding
tongue you didn't know
could fly so low. Free

of wooden feet, with not a trace
of footprint to follow
in a cold blue geological light.

If not for him, the slightest
incline would be steep
Everest.

5
While the cat-call from the gutter
daily tugs at the gut,
beneath a boneless sky poised

on mammal shoulders, only what's sleeping now
is not flying or dangerous
as the future stares

through jellied spermicides.

6
By what law then does a particle out of the vacuum
leap forth, so potent it
fractures the surface of perfect symmetry? makes

memory a backtracking river minus the living
water?—such gaffs as make us
gods to our dogs, make cicadas

clocks, make conditions for guerrilla war
even now ripen on some honeymoon shore on the planet
fueling its own ruin, hope's

inventory subtracted to zero. . . .

The self knows about zeros:
drawn through bone and marrow, the gaping

hoard of Os starved for tomorrow.

The Happiest Hope

The happiest hope has the oldest history,
the hardness of diamonds, the patience of radium.
The happiest hope buds
on the same stem where others have withered;
like the sea, it comes
                              and goes in waves.
Whoever rides it out wears the air
like a shirt that makes the wearer invisible.

The happiest hope beholds with new eyes
the jeweled constellations on the interior wall
of the inner telescope.
The happiest hope uses the same air
as everyday, and yet something else,
the way birds use the air
                              for liftoff.

The happiest hope takes its place in the ring
with the other hopes. It is granted
no privilege in that invisible hierarchy.
It does its time like the other hopes, the same,
yet something different: beholding the world
through the eyes of another, of a hundred others,
beholding the hundred worlds each of them
beholds, that each of them is . . .

The happiest hope is a hard master.
Faster than any messenger,
it feeds on the best in the worst
of possible times.

The happiest hope blends
with a phrase of Bach's, with a scent of lilac,
extracting from so sweet a tone a happiness
different if not greater than before.

The happiest hope, milky white apple blossom,
bulges on the branch, cream from the bottle.
Near us and longing
                              to be nearer.

The happiest hope weaves a spider's thread
it holds between the least chaos
and the most disaster.
                              Housing terror
the way a cloud houses the summer heat wave's
                                        wished-for rain.

The happiest hope is immaterial, like the horizon
that keeps receding. . . . So much
hope has a horizon, like a garden
you can't enter, seen from the gate.

The happiest hope pulverizes everything,
including the road we're on . . .
And the road we're on is us.
From skylark to shipwreck,
the happiest hope affirms the moment
of awareness of what there is to lose,
and redoubles its efforts in our next-to-last breath.

The happiest hope is like the moment after sunrise,
before the dew burns off,
when even the shadows on the grass sparkle.

The happiest hope is not in heaven,
but in this clawed and clawing garden
stranded like a leper among the galaxies,
abiding interstellar night that looms larger
the longer we hear no sonar beamed from the deaf-mute dark.

When the human race is ready to evolve
along other lines, the happiest hope prepares the way,
slipping in as an undertone, a foretaste
of sexual sunrise swelling at the center.

The happiest hope has its life
in your throat; when you shut your eyes you can see
right through your eyelids.

The happiest hope smells today like the grass
that long ago smelled green, the heady savor of chlorophyll,
and the air tastes as it tasted then and since then
only rarely. Air soaked in vaporized brine, the open
airing of the future coming for a taste
before its time, and being that now, that coming
change, that tunneling so rich and far
beholding what can never be held.

Whole hog, the happiest hope
is granted to no one for long.
It lies outside the reach of clocks,
where all hands are headed.
The happiest hope in the coming quake
will dance on the rolling dice of the air.

When you reach the next immobility,
the happiest hope has reached the next step.

The happiest hope rides an electron
that can be in two places at once, that can go
from here to there without going
                                in between,
and not knowing where
                    the turnoff is.
The happiest hope comes when there's nothing
to go on so that you can go anywhere
without worrying how to get back.

The happiest hope is a magic
prolonged over a lifetime, not over
in a minute.

The happiest hope, through a shell close
to the ear, tells as much as any word you say,
or meant to say between the cracks
of what is never said.

The happiest hope waits for the new life as for the morning
star, while the many wait to be one,
and the one works to be two.

The happiest hope is so sore,
when it sticks its nose out the window,
the daylight hurts it.

Where early dabs of mustard-yellow oxalis dot
the green field, the happiest
                        hope begins there.

COLOPHON

The text of this book was set in Perpetua and Klang type. Coffee House books are printed on acid free paper and smyth sewn for durablility and reading comfort.